The Coming of the Cosmic Christ

Matthew Fox

Leader's Guide

HarperSanFrancisco

A Division of HarperCollins*Publishers*

Leader's Guide prepared by Michele Idiart Walsh

FIRST EDITION

Library of Congress Cataloging-in-Publication Data for original title

Fox, Matthew.
  The coming of the cosmic Christ.

  Bibliography: p.
  Includes index
  1. Redemption.   2. Mysticism.   3. Cosmology.
  4. Human ecology—Religious aspects—Christianity.
  I. Title.   II. Title: Cosmic Christ.
  BT775.F68   1988   230   88–45136
  ISBN 0–06–062915–0 (pbk.)

ISBN 0–06–062959–2 (Leader's Guide)

91   92   93   94   95   K.P.   10   9   8   7   6   5   4   3   2   1

Starting an Adult Study Group and Using This Leader's Guide

Harper's series of Leader's Guides provides resources for small adult study groups. Each Guide is based on a widely read book by a well-known and knowledgeable author. Each provides suggestions for forming small groups and for leading the discussions. The Guides also provide discussion questions and other material that can be photocopied for participants.

Harper's Leader's Guides are designed for use in Christian churches of all denominations. However, they may also be used in other settings: neighborhood study groups, camps, retreat centers, colleges and seminaries, or continuing education classes.

Format

Harper's Leader's Guides have been planned as a basis for six one-hour sessions. Six weeks of discussion allows for depth and personal sharing, yet it is a limited commitment, one that busy adults find easier to make.

The Leader's Guides can be adapted for use in other time frames. By combining sessions, you can discuss a book in four meetings. Or, by being very selective with questions, you can plan a single two-hour session. The Guides can also serve as the foundation for a weekend retreat: the six hour-long sessions are alternated with recreation, rest, meals, and other activities.

Forming a Group

Choose a book that you think will be of interest to people in your congregation or other setting. Use your parish newsletter, announcements in services, visits to existing groups, and word of mouth to inform potential participants of the upcoming opportunity. It may be helpful to plan a brief orientation meeting for interested people.

Introduction

Each day people are bombarded by news accounts of violence, poverty, abuse of every kind, the dying environment, consumerism, and so on. Bad news seems to dominate the air waves, bringing with it a pessimism about the future. Faith in traditional approaches to these situations is waning. People are beginning to rumble about finding alternative solutions.

Matthew Fox's book *The Coming of the Cosmic Christ* comes as a fresh approach to what he terms "the dying of Mother Earth." In it he asserts that old paradigms (worldviews) are failing to address the breakdown in society, in the environment, in religion. He calls for people to embrace a "living cosmology" that links humanity with all creation and to find creative approaches to life, rooted in a deep mysticism. His book explores who the Cosmic Christ is and why a quest to discover the Cosmic Christ is essential for finding the deep bond between men and women, old and young, lifestyles, religions, nations, and time—the past, present, and the future.

Readers who come to Fox's work with an open mind will find much material to digest and to interact with. *The Coming of the Cosmic Christ* is a book to stretch with—to stretch our minds, our prejudices, ours spirits and our reponses to life. If you commit to the study of this book with openness, you will not look at the world in the same way when you are finished. You might even come up with new solutions to old problems and new hope for a weary world.

Contents

An effective discussion group can be formed with as few as three or four adults joined together by a common interest. If more than twelve people respond, they should probably be divided into smaller groups.

Participants should have access to the books at least a week before the first session. Books may be ordered through your local bookstore or from Customer Service, Harper San Francisco, 151 Union Street #401, San Francisco, CA 94111–1299, or call toll-free: 800–328–5125. Plan ahead and allow about six weeks for delivery.

At the time they receive their books, participants should also receive the material found at the back of this Leader's Guide: "Materials for Group Distribution." You may photocopy this section to hand out. You may want to distribute all of the materials initially or you may distribute the information one session at a time.

Ask participants to take time to look these over before the session. The prepared discussion questions will serve as a medium to share insights, clarify questions, and reinforce learning.

Helps for Leaders

1. Be clear in announcing the time and place of the first meeting. If possible, choose a pleasant, comfortable room in which to meet where chairs can be set in a circle. This usually encourages more discussion than a formal classroom setting does.

2. Choose a leadership style: one person may lead the discussion in all six sessions, or there may be two people who co-lead every session or who alternate sessions. Leadership may also be rotated among the participants.

3. The Leader's Guide contains several kinds of questions. Some focus on what the book says. Do not neglect these; they are basic to intelligent discussion. These are also good questions for drawing more reluctant members into the discussion. Other questions deal more with the meaning and implications of the author's words. Still others ask participants to share experiences, ideas, and feelings of their own.

4. In the Leader's Guide you will find sample responses to questions. These are not to be considered the "right answers." They are only suggested responses, which often direct you to particular passages in the book. Be open to participants' responses that may stray from these suggested answers.

5. "Materials for Group Distribution," found at the back of this Guide, can be photocopied for your group.

6. Don't feel that you have to "get through" all the questions and suggested activities in the Leader's Guide. Choose only those that seem most important to your group.

7. Try to avoid having one or two people monopolize the discussion. Call on some other participants to share their thoughts.

8. If the group spends too much time on one question, or if it goes off on a tangent, gently call it back to the topic by moving on to another question.

9. Encourage openness and trust in the group by being willing to share your own thoughts. Try to establish an atmosphere in which all ideas are treated with respect and seriousness.

10. The Leader's Guide contains some suggestions for group process. Experiment with these, and feel free to adapt them to your particular group.

Preparing for Session 1

The leader should distribute the books and discussion guides for session 1 in advance. Two options are either to give them to the participants as they register or to have a preliminary session where the plans for the sessions may be presented as well.

It is very important that the participants understand that they are to read material before each session and to answer the questions in the discussion guide. For session 1, participants should read the prologue and part 1 of *The Coming of the Cosmic Christ* and respond to questions in the discussion guide for session 1.

The group should know when and where they are to meet. Any added expectations the leader may have should also be imparted.

Two people are needed to prepare the guided reflection for session 1. Distribute to those two participants photocopies of the handout. Make sure they know which voice they will be reading; they should practice the reading before session 1.

In setting the mood or to quiet the group, reflective music can be helpful. Some possible choices include Zamfir's "Tranquility" (on Mercury) or "Harmony" (on Phillips). Steven Halpern has many tapes with environmental themes. James Galway's flute music can also be meditative. Some session closings call for participants to pass around a galaxy ball; this can be found in museum or science shops.

You should remind participants that they will need to bring paper and a pen or pencil to all sessions. It may be helpful and more convenient for each member to keep a notebook in which they record answers to discussion questions and take notes for each session.

Session 1: Our Mother Is Dying

The Coming of the Cosmic Christ, prologue and part 1

Session Objectives

- To identify expectations and preconceptions regarding Matthew Fox's book

- To explore the meaning of the phrase *your Mother is dying*

- To explore the transformation called for in embracing a living cosmology

Session Materials

- Copies of *The Coming of the Cosmic Christ*

- Extra photocopies of the discussion guide for session 1

- A Bible for each participant

- Photocopies of the discussion guide for session 2 for distribution toward the end of session 1

- A globe or galaxy ball (for the alternate closing)

Opening

Greet participants as they arrive. Be sure each has a copy of *The Coming of the Cosmic Christ* and a photocopy of discussion questions for session 1.

When the group has gathered, ask the participants to pair off with a person they do not know very well. If there is an uneven number in the group, complete the remaining pair yourself.

Give each person one minute to interview his or her partner (name, family, work, interests, etc.) in preparation for introducing the partner to the group. Next give another minute for each person to share expectations and/or preconceptions regarding Matthew

try alternate types of prayer during the week. Some suggestions are presented in the discussion guide.

If there is someone in your area experienced in contemplative prayer and mysticism, you may want to invite that person to lead the group in quiet prayer or body movement as part of your next session. If not, plan to have some reflective music, a candle, and a centering prayer to begin the next session.

Closing

Read this prayer as a closing. Ask the group to respond "Amen" to each phrase:

> *Leader:* May the Cosmic Christ redeem us from a mindless and mystic-less religion.
> *Response:* Amen.
> *Leader:* May the Cosmic Christ lead us to a saner—and less rational—century.
> *Response:* Amen.
> *Leader:* May the Cosmic Christ bless us all so that we might be blessers instead of crucifiers of Mother Earth and the generations to come.
> *Response:* Amen.

Alternate Closing: Darken the room. Pass the globe or galaxy ball around the group. As participants receive the globe, have them say the hopes they have for Mother Earth. After the last person has spoken, pause for a minute of silence.

Session 2: Resurrection Through Mysticism

The Coming of the Cosmic Christ, part 2

Session Objectives

- To explore the meaning of mysticism from two different vantage points

- To explore the differences between pseudo-mysticism and a healthy mysticism

- To explore the possibility that all human beings have the potential for mysticism, modeled on Jesus Christ

Session Materials

- Copies of *The Coming of the Cosmic Christ*

- Extra photocopies of the discussion guide for session 2

- A Bible for each participant

- A lighted candle on a table in the center of the group

- Blackboard, newsprint, or overhead projector with chalk or markers

- Meditative music (optional)

- Photocopies of the discussion guide for session 3 for distribution toward the end of session 2

Opening

Greet the participants as they arrive. Be sure each has a copy of *The Coming of the Cosmic Christ* and the photocopies of the discussion questions for session 2.

If there are new people in the group, give them time to introduce themselves. As a playful getting-to-know-you activity (and a name-memory tool), have people introduce themselves with a self-descriptive adjective that begins with the same letter as their names, for example "Mystical Mike," "Playful Pauline," "Eager Ed."

As part of their introductions, have the participants share a lifestyle change they tried during the past week as a result of session 1.

Centering Prayer: Invite your guest to lead a centering prayer. If you were not able to find someone to share quiet prayer or body movement, begin the session in a darkened room with only a lighted candle. Ask the people to close their eyes. Have them concentrate on their breathing, feeling the spirit of the Cosmic Christ flowing through them. Allow them a few minutes to quiet themselves in this way, then bring up the lights and blow out the candle before quietly moving on to "Reflecting Together."

Reflecting Together

Getting Into the Text

1. When you hear the word *mystic*, what images come to mind?

Have the participants share how they understood the word *mystic* before they read part 2 of Matthew Fox's book. Each person's response will be different. Be sure to include your own perception of *mystic* as well.

2. On a sheet of paper make a two-column chart. Head one column *Fall-Redemption* and another one *Creation-Centered Original Blessing*. Under each column head list the characteristics of each according to Fox. Then add your own comments, interpretations, and questions under each column.

On a poster sheet, blackboard, or overhead projector compile one chart from the responses of the whole group. Title the columns *Fall-Redemption* and *Creation-Centered Original Blessing*. As you record, have the participants first give their understanding of the material as Fox views it. Draw a line below this, and then have them give their responses to each one (support, question, disagreement).

The chart might look something like this:

Fall-Redemption	Creation-Centered Original Blessing
Ascetic: Mortification/ Denigration of the senses	Shut one's senses to let go of sensory input
Distrust of the body and of nature	Just to be, to awaken the senses
Patriarchal ideology of "Power over"	Basic energy/moral norm: Compassion
Enter the mysteries of the cult: Sacraments, defined as ecclesiastical liturgical rites	Primal sacrament is universe
	Calls for spiritual awakening to mysteries of the universe and our existence in it
(Participants' input)	Ascetic: spiritual athlete, engaged in mysteries of the universe, the source of all energy, rendering ritual/sacraments effective
	(Participants' input)

3. What are the effects of denying the mystic?

Fox presents the evidence of the treatment of Mother Earth and the way people treat the maternal principle as effects of the denial of the mystic. Also, he points out the depression, loneliness, youth despair, inequality, injustice, and the lack of imagination in dealing with social problems as signposts of the denial of the mystic.

4. Fox describes mysticism as "the shadow side of the Western person." What do you think he means by this?

Mysticism reflects the deeply feminist, cosmic, creation-centered and mystery-filled approach of the East, the right hemisphere of the brain. It is erotic, playful, and full of creativity. Western people tend to emphasize the values of the left brain, which appreciates analysis, work, the parts rather than the whole, dualism, power over rather than power with and in—the masculine. For balance Western people need to develop the mystical brain.

5. On another sheet list the heads *Pseudo-Mysticism*, *Today's Examples*, and *Healthy Mysticism*. Give examples of each.

On another newsprint sheet or overlay, list the examples of *Pseudo-Mysticism* and *Healthy Mysticism* in separate columns as the participants give them to you.

Responses in each column will vary. Your recording may look something like this:

Pseudo-Mysticism	Today's Examples	Healthy Mysticism
Nationalism		
Militarism		
Fascism		
Technology		
Consumerism		
Fundamentalism		
New Ageism		
Asceticism		
Mystiques		
Psychologism		

6. Fox offers twenty-one running definitions, working definitions, of mysticism. Beside each one mark your level of experience (1=never experienced, 5=faintly experienced, 10=strongly experienced). Write your own understanding of each one.

First ask the participants which of the running definitions they have strongly experienced—their 10s—and their understanding of that definition.

Then solicit from the group any definition they have faintly or never experienced. Have them include their understanding of those definitions also.

Experience	1...2...3...4...5...6...7...8...9...10
Nondualism	1...2...3...4...5...6...7...8...9...10
Compassion	1...2...3...4...5...6...7...8...9...10
Connection-Making	1...2...3...4...5...6...7...8...9...10
Radical Amazement	1...2...3...4...5...6...7...8...9...10
Affirmation of the World as a Whole	1...2...3...4...5...6...7...8...9...10
Right Brain	1...2...3...4...5...6...7...8...9...10
Self-Critical	1...2...3...4...5...6...7...8...9...10
Heart Knowledge	1...2...3...4...5...6...7...8...9...10
A Return to the Source	1...2...3...4...5...6...7...8...9...10
Feminist	1...2...3...4...5...6...7...8...9...10
Panentheistic	1...2...3...4...5...6...7...8...9...10
Birthing Images	1...2...3...4...5...6...7...8...9...10
Silence	1...2...3...4...5...6...7...8...9...10
Nothingness and Darkness	1...2...3...4...5...6...7...8...9...10
Childlike Playfulness	1...2...3...4...5...6...7...8...9...10
Psychic Justice	1...2...3...4...5...6...7...8...9...10
Prophetic	1...2...3...4...5...6...7...8...9...10
Being-With-Being	1...2...3...4...5...6...7...8...9...10
True Self	1...2...3...4...5...6...7...8...9...10
Globally Ecumenical	1...2...3...4...5...6...7...8...9...10

7. How can we test mystical claims to discern whether they are authentic or bogus? How would you apply Fox's list of tests?

The tests Fox would put to mystical claims on their authenticity are as follows:

A. Justice: more healing oneness results

B. An intellectual life: not anti-intellectual

C. Paradox and humor
D. Fertility: bears fruit
E. Unselfconsciousness: spontaneity and wonder
F. Dialectical consciousness: the ability to embrace both/and
G. Facility to experience the Cosmic Christ

Give people time to think of ways to apply Fox's list.

8. How is the historical Jesus both Mystic and Teacher of Mysticism?

Taking each of the running definitions, Fox points out how Jesus incarnated the reality. Succinctly Fox states that he believes "Jesus was a mystic in the fullest sense of the term because he lived the mystery of his relationship with the Creator and taught others to do the same. He truly 'entered the mysteries' and invited others to follow him" (pp. 72–73).

Getting Into the Heart

Let people share their thoughts and feelings on the meaning of the quotes below. Ask the participants for any other quotes from part 2 of *The Coming of the Cosmic Christ* that deepened their understanding of mysticism.

"The mystic lies deep in every person" (p. 44).

"Never devoid of mystical energy and yearnings, a society that denies the mystic and lacks a prophetic religion to insist on the primary role of the mystic within every psyche and every community, will fall into various forms of pathological pseudo-mysticisms" (p. 46).

"It remains for those who have been touched by the power of religious faith to love religion enough to criticize it" (p. 53).

"Healthy mysticism is panentheistic (all things in God and God in all things)" (p. 57).

"A prophet is a mystic in action" (p. 63).

"Without mysticism there will be no 'deep ecumenism,' no unleashing of the power of wisdom from all the world's religious traditions" (p. 65).

Personal Response and Lifestyle Choices

The discussion guide for this session suggests a number of ways participants might tap the "mystic" in them. What are their musings about their mystical being-ness?

Conclude the discussion with the following two questions.

1. "To what work and what actions does a belief in the Cosmic Christ lead?" (p. 8).

2. In response to the deepening knowledge and awareness we have gained from the study of *The Coming of the Cosmic Christ*, we will . . .

Looking Ahead

Distribute the discussion guide for session 3 to all participants and ask them to read part 3 of *The Coming of the Cosmic Christ*. To prepare for the next session, ask two or three people to volunteer to present a creative overview of the material in sections 16–18 ("Biblical Sources for Belief in the Cosmic Christ," "The Cosmic Christ and Creation Mystics—Greek Fathers," and "The Cosmic Christ and Creation Mystics—The Medieval West"). Alert the group to Fox's use of the twenty-one running definitions in part 3.

Closing:

Read this prayer from St. John of the Cross as a closing. Ask the group to respond "Although by night" to each phrase.

> *Leader:* Its source I do not know because it has none.
> And yet from this, I know, all sources come,
> *Response:* Although by night.

Leader:	I know that no created thing could be so fair
	And that both earth and heaven drink from there,
Response:	Although by night.
Leader:	Its radiance is never clouded and in this
	I know that all light has its genesis,
Response:	Although by night.
Leader:	The current welling from this fountain's source
	I know to be as mighty as its force,
Response:	Although by night.

Alternate Closing: Turn down the lights and light a candle. Quiet the participants. Ask them to let the quiet enter them.

Session 3: Questing for the Cosmic Christ

The Coming of the Cosmic Christ, part 3

Session Objectives

- To explore the scriptural and creation mystic sources for the Cosmic Christ

- To focus the paradigm shift on the quest for the Cosmic Christ (from the quest for the historical Jesus)

- To identify where the participants are in shifting their own worldviews

Session Materials

- Copies of *The Coming of the Cosmic Christ*

- Extra photocopies of the discussion guide for session 3

- Blackboard, newsprint, or overhead projector with acetates (with the appropriate chalk or markers)

- Meditative music (optional)

- Photocopies of the discussion guide for session 4 for distribution toward the end of session 3

Opening

Greet the participants as they arrive. Be sure each has a copy of *The Coming of the Cosmic Christ* and the photocopies of the discussion guide for session 3.

Have people share their names (if necessary) or have them try to remember the other participants' names and descriptive adjectives from the week before.

Have people share what comes to mind when they hear "new wine in old skins," or "new wine in fresh skins." Encourage them to relate the quotes to their own attempts to make lifestyle changes.

Introductory Comments: Since the thrust of Fox's book is to present two sides or paradigms, and to challenge readers to go on the quest for the Cosmic Christ in their lives, the material in this chapter is fundamental to understanding this book. Section 15 gives the sociological roots and ramifications for any paradigm shift. The rest of the chapter gives the foundations for shifting to the quest for the Cosmic Christ. The focus of this session is first to understand Kuhn's process of paradigm shifting and to identify a time in the participants' lives when they have questioned their worldview and have had to let go and move on. The second part is to explore the foundations in Scripture and patristic and medieval literature for the Cosmic Christ.

Reflecting Together

Getting Into the Text

1. Describe what Fox feels the Enlightenment and Augustine have bequeathed to the people of the West.

According to Fox the Enlightenment deposed the Cosmic Christ and banished mystery and mysticism. Rationalism and pietism infiltrated Christianity. Augustine bequeathed a pre-occupation with guilt and salvation and an anthropocentric spirituality. Since the time of the Enlightenment, the West lost its mystical tradition (the Cosmic Christ) and went on a search for the historical Jesus.

2. In the quest for the Cosmic Christ what paradigms or worldviews does Fox say we have to get rid of? What does this mean to you, and how do you feel about it?

Fox says that the quest for the Cosmic Christ involves letting go of the old paradigms of education and theology, of an anthropocentric, rationalistic, antimystical, antimaternal worldview.

Ask the participants to give their own meaning to Fox's comments and to share their feelings about it.

3. Weight Kuhn's descriptions of the new paradigm ("10" being the one that best expresses your experience of vision or life shifts in your own life and "1" being the one that least expresses it). Give your reason for your choices.

Have people share how they weighted Kuhn's descriptions of the new paradigm and their reasons for their choices.

See nature in a new way	1...2...3...4...5...6...7...8...9...10
A shift of vision	1...2...3...4...5...6...7...8...9...10
A transformation of vision	1...2...3...4...5...6...7...8...9...10
A conversion	1...2...3...4...5...6...7...8...9...10
A map or directions for making a map	1...2...3...4...5...6...7...8...9...10
A switch in a visual gestalt	1...2...3...4...5...6...7...8...9...10

4. According to Kuhn what is the process of shifting from one worldview to another? What is required for people involved in a paradigm shift?

According to Kuhn the origin of the shift is an anomaly (something that causes a person or society to stop the normal routine), awakening that person or society to new questions, to the realization that something is amiss. This awakening, if responded to, leads to a breakthrough.

The second step is a crisis or breakdown (a failure to fit) in the old paradigm.

After the breakdown there is a transition period when both paradigms are operative in the person or society and the person or society fluctuates between two decisively different ways of solving problems.

Moving through the process will lead to a redefinition and revolution of worldview and paradigms. Because resistance and denial often accompany a shift, participating in the shift requires generosity, courage, and sacrifice.

5. What are the six categories in the New Testament that alert you to the presence of the Cosmic Christ? Choose one of the texts that Fox suggests (infancy narratives, transfiguration, resurrection, etc.—see pp. 99–107) and reread this Scripture in light of these six categories. What has happened to your understanding and awareness of the events in Jesus' life?

Matthew Fox suggests we reread the Scriptures mindful of six categories that will alert us to the presence of the Cosmic Christ: angels, Lord, cloud, glory, wilderness and mountains, and evil.

Have people share the insights they gained in rereading the Scripture they chose.

Notice that Fox is not calling for throwing out the historical Jesus—the historical Jesus, he believes, taught us to be Cosmic Christs as he was. It is the theological quest for the historical Jesus that is mostly completed at this time in history.

6. After reading sections 16–19, what was your familiarity with the literature from the Wisdom or Cosmic Christ Tradition: very familiar, somewhat familiar, or unfamiliar?

Each person's response will be different.

7. Drawing from the biblical, patristic, and medieval sources, come up with your own description of the Cosmic Christ.

Each person's description and media will be different. Some possible descriptions might be "Eternal Word," "Cosmic Wisdom," "Lover," "Pulsating Life Force."

8. Make a two-column chart. Label one column *Historical Jesus* and the other *Cosmic Christ*. Write their particular characteristics in the appropriate column.

Begin two charts that will be continued in future sessions. Title one *Historical Jesus* and the other *Cosmic Christ*.

Under each title write the particular characteristics. In the next sessions the group will add other characteristics and the ramifications for social justice, sexuality, liturgy, and prayer that they see.

Historical Jesus	*Cosmic Christ*
Man	"Neither Jew nor Greek, slave nor
Jew in Palestine	free, male nor female."
First Century	Eternal, Infinite, Pre-existing
Image of the Godhead	Godhead present in all
Localized	Universalized
Teaches how to be "image of God" or Cosmic Christ	The object of Jesus' teaching (Other contributions)
(Other contributions)	

Getting Into the Heart

If you had people prepare a creative overview of the material on the biblical, patristic and medieval sources on the Cosmic Christ, have them present it.

If not, let people share their reflections (thoughts and feelings) on the quotes listed below. Ask the participants to contribute any other quotes from the sources that deepened their understanding of the Cosmic Christ.

" 'Am I a God close at hand, and not a God far off?' says the Lord. 'Can anyone hide oneself in secret places where I shall not see them? Do I not fill heaven and earth?' says the Lord" (Jer. 23:23–24).

"The word of Yahweh was addressed to me, saying, 'Before I formed you in the womb I knew you, before you came to birth I consecrated you; I have appointed you a prophet to the nations'" (Jer. 1:4–5).

"He is the image of the invisible God, the first-born of all creation; for in him all things were created, in heaven and on earth, visible and invisible, whether thrones or dominions or principalities or authorities—all things were created through him and for him. He is before all things, and in him all things hold together. He is the first-born from the dead, that in everything he might be preeminent. For in him all the fullness of God was pleased to dwell, and through him to reconcile to himself all things, whether on earth or in heaven, making peace by his death on the cross" (Col. 1:15–20).

"In the beginning was the Word: the Word was with God and the Word was God. This Word was with God in the beginning. Through it all things came to be, not one thing had its being but through it. All that came to be had life in it . . ." (John 1:1–4).

"God became a human being in order that human beings might become God" (Iranaeus in Fox, p. 109).

"The Logos of God has become human so that you might learn from a human being how a human being may become divine" (Clement of Alexandria in Fox, p. 109).

"Every creature participates in some way in the likeness of the Divine Essence" (Thomas Aquinas in Fox, p. 115).

"When are we like God? I will tell you. In so far as we love compassion and practice it steadfastly, to that extent do we resemble the heavenly Creator who practices these things ceaselessly in us" (Mechtild in Fox, p. 118).

"I saw a great oneing between Christ and us because when he was in pain we were in pain. All creatures of God's creation that can suffer pain suffered with him. The sky and the earth failed at the time of Christ's dying because he too was part of nature" (Julian of Norwich in Fox, p. 124).

Personal Responses and Lifestyle Choices
Give the participants time to share their personal responses to "shift experiences" in their own lives and in the world.

Personal Paradigm Shifts

1.   Identify a time in your life when you were stopped in your regular routine or relationship patterns. Describe the experience.

2.   What new questions arose from the experience? What went amiss?

3.   What resulted from the breakdown (failure to fit)?

4.   Did you try to hold onto the "old way"? Why or why not?

5.   Did you waver between the "old" and "new" ways of responding or relating?

Societal Paradigm Shifts

1.   Where in the world or universe are there anomalies (breakdowns) where old answers or practices are not working?

2.   What new questions do these anomalies raise for you?

3.   How do you think a belief in the Cosmic Christ might address these experiences?

4.   What does the Cosmic Christ call for in these experiences?

Lead the group to come up with some lifestyle choices as a result of their study of part 3 of *The Coming of the Cosmic Christ*.

1.   "To what work and what actions does a belief in the Cosmic Christ lead?" (p. 8)

2.   In response to the deepening knowledge and awareness we have gained from the study of *The Coming of the Cosmic Christ*, we will . . .

Looking Ahead

Distribute the discussion guide for session 4 to all participants and ask them to read part 4 of *The Coming of the Cosmic Christ*. To prepare for the next session, have the participants make a list of titles or names for Jesus Christ.

Closing

Reflectively read the words of Julian of Norwich (Fox, pp. 123–24) and have the participants respond "Come, Lord Jesus Christ" after each phrase.

Leader:	Our Lord Jesus oftentimes said: "This I am. This I am."
Response:	Come, Lord Jesus Christ.
Leader:	"I am what you love."
Response:	Come, Lord Jesus Christ.
Leader:	"I am what you enjoy."
Response:	Come, Lord Jesus Christ.
Leader:	"I am what you serve."
Response:	Come, Lord Jesus Christ.
Leader:	"I am what you long for."
Response:	Come, Lord Jesus Christ.
Leader:	"I am what you desire."
Response:	Come, Lord Jesus Christ.
Leader:	"I am what you intend."
Response:	Come, Lord Jesus Christ.
Leader:	"I am all that is."
Response:	Come, Lord Jesus Christ.

Alternate closing: Read reflectively the words of Elisabeth Schüssler Fiorenza: "According to Revelation, final salvation does not just pertain to the soul and spiritual realities. It is the abolishment of all dehumanization and suffering and at the same time the fullness of human well-being . . . a rectification of the great tribulation with its sufferings of war, peacelessness, hunger, and inflation, pestilence, persecution, and death" (Fox, p. 98).

Session 4: The Challenge of the Cosmic Christ

The Coming of the Cosmic Christ, part 4

Session Objectives

- To discuss who the Cosmic Christ is to us
- To have the participants explore the names of the Cosmic Christ in relation to their own lives

Session Materials

- Copies of *The Coming of the Cosmic Christ*
- Extra photocopies of the discussion guide for session 4
- A Bible for each participant
- Blackboard, newsprint, or overhead projector with acetates (with the appropriate chalk or markers)
- The Historical Jesus and Cosmic Christ charts from session 3
- Meditative music (optional)
- Photocopies of the discussion guide for session 5 for distribution toward the end of session 4

Opening

Greet the participants as they arrive. Be sure each has a copy of *The Coming of the Cosmic Christ* and the photocopies of the discussion guide for session 4.

Have the participants share their list of titles or names for Jesus Christ. Talk together about these titles and names; what are their purposes and power?

Reflecting Together

Getting Into the Text

1.   What are the differences between a mindless (unhealthy) and a mindful (healthy) religion?

According to Fox a mindless (unhealthy) religion is one that is sentimental and anti-intellectual. It lacks cosmology. A mindful (healthy) religion creates mindfulness, opening and awakening minds and hearts to the universe. It calls participants to the divinity around them and sees people and other creatures as joint citizens of a vast history and universe.

2.   "How can religion accomplish this task of mindfulness?" (p. 132).

One way is to take in the wisdom of the scientists who explore the universe and then to explain to people what is, to interpenetrate science and mysticism.

Give the participants an opportunity to share their answers to the question.

3.   Fox names the Cosmic Christ "The Pattern that Connects." What does he mean?

The Cosmic Christ insists on the interconnectivity of all things: our knowledge and love of the universe/our moral behavior, connection/disconnection, death/resurrection, heaven/earth, past/future, divinity/humanity, all of creation.

4.   Using the new wineskin imagery, Fox says that the new paradigm of the Cosmic Christ ushers in a call for a new lifestyle (a connecting, coherent wineskin). What connections do you see the Cosmic Christ making?

Some ideas might be our connections to the universe, to the earth; a connection to oneself (body, head, heart); a connection to *all* people; a connection to God in all; a connection to the past (ancestors and communion of saints) and the future; and so on.

5. Fox says that the Cosmic Christ demands a paradigm shift from one worldview to another. Translate his list into one that relates to your experience. Make a four-column chart. Head the first column *Fox's From . . .* , the second column *Fox's To . . .* , the third column *My From . . .* , and the last *My To . . . .* Fill in the columns.

Do you understand and accept Fox's list? Do you have any questions or misgivings about it?

Create a chart with four columns. Label them: *Fox's From . . . , Fox's To . . . , Our From . . . ,* and *Our To . . . .* As the people in the group give their responses, fill them in under the appropriate title. For example:

Fox's From . . .	Fox's To . . .	Our From . . .	Our To . . .
Anthropo-centrism	A living cosmology	Man as center and end of the universe	Human beings as part of a larger universe
Newton	Einstein		
Parts mentality	Wholeness		
Rationalism	Mysticism		
Obedience as prime moral virtue	Creativity as prime moral virtue		
Personal salvation	Communal healing (compassion as salvation)		
Theism (God outside)	Panentheism (God in us & us in God)		
Fall-redemption religion	Creation-centered spirituality		
Ascetic	Aesthetic		

If the participants do not understand or agree with Fox's list, take time to discuss their questions or misgivings.

6. What do you think Fox means when he says, "The Cosmic Christ is not born yet"?

Fox seems to mean that Jesus Christ handed over the coming of the reign of God to "other Christs" who are to birth justice, order, harmony, peace; to increase the glory of the divine presence in the cosmos as he did. He promised to send the Spirit to assist others to imitate him.

7. What are the two persons Jesus became for us? What do his followers become?

First Jesus is the crucified one who lives in all people, and second he is the power of the mystical life pumping in all people. His followers become "other Christs," bearers of the image of the Cosmic Christ.

8. What allusions does Fox use to align Jesus Christ with Mother Earth? What does he hope will ensue from this new symbol?

Jesus is described as the sun, the light. He is crucified, yet rising, as Mother Earth is wounded, yet called to rise. Jesus likens himself to a mother hen gathering her chicks, weeping for his inability to protect. Jesus is called "first fruits."

Ask the group if they can think of other allusions that connect Jesus with Mother Earth.

Symbolizing Jesus as Mother Earth has the potential to awaken humans to the survival of Mother Earth, to the elimination of matricide, and to people's awareness of their best selves as mystics, prophets, and creative persons. It has the potential to launch a global spirituality, awakening people to their oldest and deepest traditions (a living cosmology) and uniting them with other persons of good will.

9. What is the "paschal mystery for the Third Millennium"?

It is the life, death, and resurrection of Mother Earth in which the Christian Church and sacrament can be reborn.

10. Which of the eleven descriptive names Fox gives to the Cosmic Christ resonate in you? Why?

Have the participants share the names Fox gives to the Cosmic Christ that resonate for them and why.

Creator of Mindfulness

Pattern that Connects

Bearer of Coherence

Needing to Be Born

One Birth, One Death, One Work

Connector of Time and Space

Connector of Microcosm and Macrocosm

Mother Earth Crucified and Resurrected

Paschal Mystery for the Third Millennium of Christianity

Redeemer of the Cosmic Pain

Revealer of the Divine "I Am" in Every Creature

Bring back the charts from session 3 with *Historical Jesus* and *Cosmic Christ* on them. Add the descriptive names for the Cosmic Christ from this chapter.

Have the participants recall the names and titles of Jesus Christ that they shared at the beginning of this session. Have participants decide whether each name or title would fit the historical Jesus or the Cosmic Christ. Add them to the appropriate chart.

Getting Into the Heart

Continue with the *Historical Jesus/Cosmic Christ* charts. On each chart add another column entitled "Challenge." In this column have the participants put what they see the challenge to be for someone who accepts each title or name. Remind the participants of the "I-am-ness" that Fox sees coming with accepting a name or title, for example: for the title "Pattern that Connects," the participants reflect on the challenge of saying, "I am the pattern that connects," and so on.

Let the participants share their thoughts and feelings about the quotes below. Ask them for any other quotes that deepened their understanding of the Cosmic Christ.

"Divine am I inside and out, and I make holy whatever I touch or
    am touched from.
Why should I wish to see God better than this day?
. . . .
I see something of God each hour of the twenty-four, and each
    moment then,
In the faces of men and women I see God, and in my own face
    in the glass;
I find letters from God dropped in the street, and every one is
    signed by God's name" (Walt Whitman in Fox, p. 130).

"Belief is not belief if it is not launched into *praxis*" (p. 134).

"[. . . because of the incarnation the human is involved] in a new responsibility. He can no longer wiggle out of it on the plea of his littleness and nothingness, for the dark God has slipped the atom bomb and chemical weapons into his hands and given him the power to empty out the apocalyptic vials of wrath on his fellow creatures. Since he has been granted an almost godlike power, he can no longer remain blind and unconscious. He must know something of God's nature and of metaphysical processes if he is to understand himself and thereby achieve gnosis of the Divine" (Carl Jung in Fox, p. 138).

"The earth should not be injured, the earth should not be destroyed. As often as the elements of the world are violated by ill-treatment, so God will cleanse them. God will cleanse them through the sufferings, through the hardships of humankind. All of creation God gives to humankind to use. But if this privilege is misused, God's justice permits creation to punish humanity" (Hildegard of Bingen in Fox, p. 144).

"Salvation is understood as liberation from bondage" (p. 150).

"The Good News we yearn to hear and that Mother Earth herself yearns to feel is that salvation is about solidarity: solidarity with God, neighbor, and all God's creatures. The idea of private salvation is obsolete" (p. 151).

"Our capacity for the universe is both divine and demonic, both positive and negative, both glory and shadow" (p. 152).

"Wherever injustice reigns the Cosmic Christ is crucified again. This also means that wherever justice is fought for and prevails; wherever healing takes place and is passed on; wherever compassion prevails, the Cosmic Christ is healing redeeming, liberating on a cosmic scale. The Cosmic Christ leads the way to cosmic redemption" (p. 153).

Personal Response and Lifestyle Choices

Give the participants an opportunity to share their creative naming of the Cosmic Christ. Each participant has the opportunity to use a creative medium to name the Cosmic Christ (poetry, dance, drawing, painting, song, humor, etc.).

Lead the group to come up with some lifestyle choices as a result of their study of part 4 of *The Coming of the Cosmic Christ*. Have participants share any lifestyle changes they have attempted as a result of their study of Fox's book.

1.   "To what work and what actions does a belief in the Cosmic Christ lead?" (p. 8)

2.   In response to the deepening knowledge and awareness of the "I-am-ness" of the Cosmic Christ, we will . . .

Looking Ahead

Distribute the discussion guide for session 5 to all participants and ask them to read part 5 of *The Coming of the Cosmic Christ*. Ask some people to prepare a creative reflection on the healing called for in Walt Whitman's quote, "If life and the soul are sacred the human body is sacred" (in Fox, p. 157). A creative reflection can be dance, body movement, a poem, or song.

Closing

Take the titles and names for the Cosmic Christ that the group surfaced. Read each one aloud. After each one have the group respond "come." After the final one the response will be "Cosmic Christ, come."

Alternate Closing: Reflectively read the words of Kabir: "Who is a holy person? The one who is aware of others' suffering" (Kabir in Fox, p. 131).

Session 5: Healing Mother Earth

The Coming of the Cosmic Christ, part 5

Session Objectives

- To explore Fox's call for healing of Mother Earth and a global renaissance

- To assess Fox's suggestions for bringing about this healing and renaissance

- To identify how group members can participate in the healing of Mother Earth and in the global renaissance

Session Materials

- Copies of *The Coming of the Cosmic Christ*

- Extra photocopies of the discussion guide for session 5

- A Bible for each participant

- Blackboard, newsprint, or overhead projector with acetates (with appropriate chalk or markers)

- The *Historical Jesus/Cosmic Christ* charts from last session

- Meditative music (for the closing)

- Photocopies of the discussion guide for session 6 for distribution toward the end of session 5.

Opening

Greet the participants as they arrive. Be sure each has a copy of *The Coming of the Cosmic Christ* and the photocopies of the discussion guide for session 5.

Have the participants share their creative reflection on the healing called for in Walt Whitman's quote, "If life and the soul are sacred the human body is sacred" (in Fox, p. 157).

If no one is prepared to respond creatively, take a few minutes to discuss the quote as an introduction to Fox's material in part 5.

Reflecting Together

Because part 5 of *The Coming of the Cosmic Christ* is so rich in ideas, you may want to extend discussion of this into session 6. Allow for this possibility.

Getting Into the Text

1. Fox asks, "Is the human race still capable ... of a new birth from a spiritual initiative?" (p. 160). Mark your response to that question and give your reason.

1. . . . . 2. . . . . 3. . . . . 4. . . . . 5. . . . . 6. . . . . 7. . . . . 8. . . . . 9. 10
No   Maybe   Yes

Allow the participants time to share their responses and their reasons.

2. Fox says that the West's teaching on sexuality has been marked by silence and moralizing, leaving a message of regret. What does he mean by those statements? Do you agree with his assessment?

By silence Fox means that there are no puberty rites, rites of passage for the young to celebrate the news that they are fit and able to pass on the mystery of human life. Moralizing takes over when people are told of the sins they are capable of performing with their sexuality. The message of regret is sounded in phrases like "If only sexuality would go away, we could get on with important issues of faith."

Give the participants an opportunity to share whether they agree with Fox's statements on sexuality.

3. In contrast to the West's teaching on sexuality, Fox presents the sexual mysticism of the Song of Songs. What are the

elements of sexual mysticism Fox sees present in the Song of Songs? Do you agree or disagree with the perspective on sexuality in the Song of Songs?

Make a list of the elements as the participants share them. When you have finished, have them give their opinions on the ones with which they agree or disagree.

An essential element in sexual mysticism is a sense of personhood—"isness," "I-am-ness." Another is fidelity, being faithful, patient, and committed to mutual exploration. Fox sees infidelity as an offense against the Cosmic Christ radiating from one's lover. Another element is that to be in love is to be in love with the whole person. The Song of Songs also sees lovers existing in a universe, not just in their personal relationship. To make love is to enter into the "cosmological wilderness," to the darkness where God speaks heart-to-heart. To make love is to play again in the universe, to make laughter and sabbath together. The Song of Songs also explores the cosmic pain and vulnerability that the absence of the beloved brings, the power to make the lovers suffer deprivation and loss, wounds, and misunderstanding. Sexual love hints of our own mortality, so that in sexual ecstasy the finite and the infinite are both tasted.

4. Fox states that the female and male actors in the Song of Songs do not play out stereotypical roles. What does he mean by this statement? Do you agree?

The woman is assertive, certain of her own "I-am-ness." She is fully the equal of man. The man is patient, respectful of the natural needs and rhythms of his beloved—not rapacious, possessive, demanding, or controlling. The man and woman are mature lovers seeking one another's pleasure as well as their own.

Ask the members of your group if they agree with Fox's analysis.

5. Fox asserts that the problems with today's youth are caused by adultism (excessive adult self-interest). Rate your agreement with his assertion.

Strongly Disagree	Disagree	Unsure	Agree	Strongly Agree

Ask the group about their level of agreement with Fox's statement about the cause of problems with today's youth.

6. In Section 26 Fox describes modern society as Chronos. What does he mean? What is the role of Christos?

Modern society is characterized by its consumerism and waste, thus modeling itself after the god Chronos, the ultimate consumer and waster. Jealousy, fear, competitiveness, and resentment of the young result.

The Christos loves the children and represents the youthfulness of God. Christos sacrifices himself for his children. He brings wisdom and reverence.

7. In a healthy psyche and culture, Senex (the old) and Puer (the young) work together. What are the healthy aspects of each? Why are both necessary? Make a two-column chart. Head one *Senex* and the other *Puer*. Under each, list its healthy aspects.

Senex	*Puer*
"the old eye"—distance, depth, essence, wisdom	Resurrection—something new happening
In touch with living traditions (mysticism and cosmology)	Awe and Wonder
	Play
Sees significance of stories from past for the now	Need to revolt, to assert its individuality
Able to pass stories on	Nowness
Knows enemies from the past and battles that have been waged	Wanderlust
	Unselfconsciousness
Passionate about future	Wants to soar, to experience mysticism
Awareness of eschatology (last things)	

Both Senex and Puer are necessary for balance, for connections, for wholeness.

8. Fox states that the Cosmic Christ will awaken "the divine powers of creativity in all persons" (p. 199). Where does he see creativity happening? What part of Fox's presentation on creativity excited you? Why?

The awakening of creativity will happen within individuals themselves as they take more responsibility for birthing their own personalities, lifestyles, relationships, and citizenship. It will happen in folk art, play, work, and education.

Ask the participants to share what excited them in Fox's presentation on creativity.

9. "What are the personal arts that we all need to start birthing anew?" (p. 200). What value do you put on them?

The personal arts include the art of friendship, the art of making beauty where we dwell, the arts of conversation, massage, laughter, preparing food, hospitality, the sharing of ideas, growing food and flowers, singing songs, making love, telling stories, uniting generations, putting on skits, satirizing human folly. They also include the arts of listening and healing, enjoying oneself with others in simple ways; the art of creating our lifestyles and our communities; the art of conviviality; the arts of parenting and of forgiving.

10. Fox gives six steps to revitalizing worship. Evaluate his list by making "1" least important and "10" most important (vital).

Reset all of worship in a cosmological context.	1. . .2. . .3. . .4. . .5. . .6. . .7. . .8. . .9. . .10
Bring the body back.	1. . .2. . .3. . .4. . .5. . .6. . .7. . .8. . .9. . .10
Bring play back.	1. . .2. . .3. . .4. . .5. . .6. . .7. . .8. . .9. . .10
Make room for Via Negativa, darkness, silence, suffering.	1. . .2. . .3. . .4. . .5. . .6. . .7. . .8. . .9. . .10

Awaken and nurture   1...2...3...4...5...6...7...8...9...10
the prophet.

Bring participation back.   1...2...3...4...5...6...7...8...9...10

Ask the participants about their current experiences of worship. Then have them rate their experiences of worship using these same six criteria.

11. What are the lessons Fox says can be learned from native worship? Would you add these lessons to your steps in revitalizing worship? Why or why not?

Fox says that native peoples see sacrifice (denying oneself something in order to prepare for worship) as essential. Gratitude motivates their worship, and community is a vital element. An invitation to bravery and heroism is presented to all the participants in native worship. Also the twenty-one running definitions of mysticism are present.

Ask your group if they would add these lessons from native worship to their steps in revitalizing worship. How would they do this?

12. Fox presents the challenge to bring about deep ecumenism based in mysticism. What do you think are the ramifications of accepting that challenge for world religions, education, and justice?

Some responses might be: world religions, rooted in mysticism, would begin to see the oneness of people's search and to work together for peace. All life will be seen as connected because of its place in the universe. Education would stress this oneness and unity, leading people to treasure the wisdom and stories of the old and the vision and adventure of the young. Deep mysticism will establish right relationships in the universe. In time and space there will be healing of all injustice. A common language would emerge. Artists would be employed to express this deep experience.

13. Is the term *Cosmic Christ* anti-ecumenical?

The concept of the Cosmic Christ is pre-Christian, set deep in the Jewish tradition of wisdom. Scientists also talk about the living reality that is total and unbroken and undivided in everything, the "is-ness" of being that is divine. Fox names that reality the Cosmic Christ. *Christos* suggests a person who has been anointed: royalty patterned after the royal dignity of the Creator; prophet who brings compassion and justice for those who have no voice. Anointing with oil symbolizes making smooth, limiting friction, lubricating. The Cosmic Christ comes to make connections, to minimize friction and to build community among all peoples. If the title "Cosmic Christ" carries too much baggage, Fox offers the title "Cosmic Wisdom," which bears the same meaning.

Getting Into the Heart

Let people share their reflections (thoughts and feelings) on the meaning of the quotes cited below. Ask the participants for any other quotes that deepened their understanding of the healing and renaissance that the Cosmic Christ will bring.

"Both religion and sexuality heal the split between ourselves and the universe. We discover that we are indeed 'part of everything' and one with the mystery of life. To talk about God in relation to our sexuality means to be aware of love moving in us, for 'in God we live and move and have our being'" (Dorothee Soelle in Fox, p. 157).

"[We] need to 'reinvent the human'" (Thomas Berry in Fox, p. 160).

"We need today *a historical Christ*—a living Christ who can change history once again and ground that change in a living cosmology" (p. 162).

"How are we treating our young? Are we preparing them to love life? Are we offering them skills and disciplines for adventure, for sacrifice, for great visions to which they can give themselves?" (p. 181).

"Living worship, based on a living cosmology, creates a people and heals a people; it celebrates a people and their amazing place in the universe" (p. 212).

". . . I'm convinced that the only way to survive nuclear roulette is to stop playing the game, to put down the gun globally, to move beyond war. If we want to avoid the world's imminent suicide, we must shift totally the way we think about war. We no longer can accept it as a means of settling disputes, as an extension of politics or as an innate ingredient in the nature of man" (Martin Heldman in Fox, p. 234).

"Religious traditions hold collective power—especially because they are more in touch with the *anawim* or voiceless ones—to motivate governments to interact on behalf of peace and justice" (p. 235).

"The Cosmic Christ still needs to be born in all of us—no individual, race, religion, culture, or time is excluded. 'Christ' is a generic name. In that sense we are all 'other Christs'" (p. 235).

Personal Response and Lifestyle Choices

Give the group time to share their personal responses to being "other Christs."

1. **For me to be another Christ means . . .**

2. **The deep healing that I believe needs to happen is . . .**

Lead the group to come up with some lifestyle choices as a result of their study of part 5 of *The Coming of the Cosmic Christ.*

3. **"To what work and what actions does a belief in the Cosmic Christ lead?" (p. 8)**

4. **In response to the deepening knowledge and awareness of our being "other Christs," I will . . .**

Looking Ahead

Distribute the discussion guide for session 6 to all participants and ask them to read the Epilogue. Encourage them to review *The Coming of the Cosmic Christ*.

Two possible strategies are offered for "Getting Into the Heart" in session 6. Alert the participants to the possibilities for your next discussion and have them decide with you which would be the most helpful. Encourage them to do the background preparation for the strategy they have chosen.

In both strategies, participants are divided into two groups and these groups are assigned one of four "neighborhoods" described on the session 6 discussion guide. You will want to divide the group into two now. Assign one of the groups a neighborhood that is similar to its own. Give the other group one that is different from its own.

In strategy one the groups will brainstorm responses to the background questions. Their discussion in your next session will be on their neighborhood's response to the announcement that the Cosmic Christ is coming.

In strategy two the groups also brainstorm responses to the background questions. Then they dramatize scenarios that would cause each neighborhood to reconsider its present worldview. The groups will give the background to the scenario and then role play the responses of different people in the neighborhood.

Closing

Stand and form a circle. Join hands or link arms. Play music that puts the group in touch with the universe—music with a global or cosmological message. Begin to move with the music. (Some possible music choices are Paul Winter's "Earth: Voices for a Planet" or his "Concert for the Earth.")

Alternate Closing: Reflectively read the Cosmic Christ's call to renewed worship on pp. 227–28:

Come to me all you who are burdened by lack of praise, lack of beauty, lack of vision in your lives. Look about you at the starry heavens and the deep, deep sea; at the amazing history that has birthed a home for you on this planet; at the surprise and joy of your existence. Gather together—you and your communities—in the context of this great, cosmic community to rejoice and give thanks. To heal and let go. To enter the dark and deep mysteries, to share the news, to break the bread of the universe and drink blood of the Cosmos itself in all its divinity. Be brave. Let your worship make you strong and great again. Never be bored again. Create yourselves, re-create your worlds, by the news you share and the visions you celebrate. Bring your sense of being microcosm in vast macrocosm; bring your bodies; bring your play; bring your darkness and your pain. Gather and do not scatter. Learn not to take for granted and learn this together. Become a people. Worship together.

Session 6: Am I Ready for the Cosmic Christ?

Review *The Coming of the Cosmic Christ* and read the Epilogue.

Session Objectives

- To review *The Coming of the Cosmic Christ*
- To apply the Cosmic Christ to life situations
- To evaluate Fox's dream
- To have the participants say how they will respond to the coming of the Cosmic Christ

Session Materials

- Copies of *The Coming of the Cosmic Christ*
- Extra photocopies of the discussion guide for session 6
- A Bible for each participant
- A candle on the table in the center of the group
- Blackboard, newsprint, or overhead projector with acetates (with the appropriate chalk or markers)
- The charts or acetates from previous sessions
- Meditative music (optional)
- A globe or galaxy ball (for closing)

Opening

Greet the participants as they arrive. Be sure each has a copy of *The Coming of the Cosmic Christ* and the photocopies of the discussion guide for session 6. Prepare the group for the gathering activities by telling them the session will begin in darkness with time for silence.

Gathering Activity: Darken the room and quiet the group. Ask participants to concentrate on their breathing.

Allow two to three minutes of silence. Let the silence surround, penetrate, and fill the room.

Begin to pass the globe or galaxy ball around the darkened room. Let each person hold it awhile in silence.

Pass it a second time; this time encourage each person to share how he or she experiences the dying of Mother Earth.

After everyone has had a chance to share, take the globe or galaxy ball and place it in the center of the group.

Light the candle and allow a few minutes for silent reflection. Bring up the lights, blow out the candle, and gently move on to discussion.

Reflecting Together

Complete the discussion of material from part 5 of Fox as necessary before moving into the following review discussion.

Getting Into the Text

Bring the charts from all previous sessions. Retitle them "Fox's View." Make a new chart with "Our View" on top to answer the following questions.

1. After your study of Fox's book, write a description of mysticism's place in the coming of the Cosmic Christ.

Your group's description will reflect their own perceptions of mysticism. Review Fox's presentation on mysticism to be able to give input.

2. Who is the Cosmic Christ?

Remembering Jesus' question "Who do you say that I am?" give time for each person to share who the Cosmic Christ is for them.

3. What paradigm shift do you feel must happen in society and/or the church? Why? Do you think the environment exists for this shift to happen?

Again each person may have a different view. Respect the different responses.

4. What is the most important message of the Cosmic Christ for you? Why?

Each person's important message may be different.

5. What are the ramifications for a person who believes in the Cosmic Christ—lifestyle, education, social and ecumenical responsibilities, and so on? What are the ramifications for a church or society?

Responses might center around unity with all creation, oneness with all people, and within each person; education for life, balance between right and left brain; psychic and social justice; and so on.

Getting Into the Heart

In this section background data is offered for four imaginary but possible neighborhoods. Take them as they are or adapt them to your experience. Two possible strategies are offered for your group to deal with this data. Choose one that will be the most helpful to get into the heart of Fox's material.

In both strategies, participants are divided into two groups and these groups are assigned one of the four "neighborhoods" described here and on the discussion guides for session 6. One group should be assigned a neighborhood that is similar to its own. Give the other group one that is different from its own. Initially the groups will brainstorm responses to the background questions regarding their assigned neighborhoods. After that, if strategy one has been chosen, the groups will focus their discussions on their neighborhood's response to the announcement that the Cosmic Christ is coming. If strategy two has been chosen, groups will dramatize scenarios causing their neighborhood to change its worldview.

Neighborhood 1: Inner Suburbia or Rural
- Stable neighborhood (15+ years)
- Moderate income
- Two parents, 3–8+ children
- Husband works outside the home; wife at home; if farm, everyone works
- White
- Churchgoers
- (Add other characteristics to flesh out this neighborhood)

Neighborhood 2: Outer Suburbia
- Mobile neighborhood (3–5 years)
- Moderate income (middle to upper middle)
- Mixed families (single- and two-parent); 1–3 children
- Two incomes usually
- Mixed backgrounds (ethnic, educational, economic, religious, etc.)
- Mixed level of church involvement
- (Add other characteristics to flesh out this neighborhood)

Neighborhood 3: Inner Urban
- Stable neighborhood (feeling of being stuck here by many)
- Lower income level
- Mixed families (leaning toward more single-parent families); 3–8 children
- Usually single income, welfare a reality for many
- Mixed backgrounds—black, Hispanic, and new immigrants with some whites
- For many the church is a respite in a bleak experience, a connection with their mother country; for others it is another oppressor
- (Add other characteristics to flesh out this neighborhood)

Neighborhood 4: Outer Urban
- Mobile neighborhood (many renters)
- Middle to upper middle income, some wealthy
- Mixed lifestyles (single- and two-parent families, homosexual singles and couples)
- Single and double incomes

- Mixed backgrounds (ethnic, educational, economic, religious, etc.)
- Mixed level of church involvement (from alienation to full participation)
- (Add other characteristics to flesh out this neighborhood)

Brainstorm Background Questions (in a real, not ideal, setting)

1.   **Family Decisions: Who makes them, how are they made (process, criteria), who is accountable, who affected? Who is welcome or acceptable in the family? What is the level of trust? What is it based on?**

2.   **Neighborhood and Civic Decisions: Who makes them, how are they made (process, criteria), who is accountable, who affected? Who is welcome or accepted in the neighborhood or civic community? What is the level of trust? What is it based on?**

3.   **Church Decisions (if applicable): Who makes them, how are they made (process, criteria), who is accountable, who affected? Who is welcome or accepted in the church? What is the level of trust? What is it based on?**

4.   **Describe what sexuality, morality, creativity, play, work, and worship look like in the neighborhood. What place does each one have in the life of the people?**

5.   **Describe how the neighborhood feels about the government, the military, social programs.**

6.   **What would cause each neighborhood to reconsider its present worldview?**

Strategy One: The Cosmic Christ Is Coming!
(Use your imagination, creativity, your right brain as well as the content from Fox's presentation to approach these questions.)

1.   **Will your neighborhood welcome the Cosmic Christ? Why or Why not? What would it take for it to recognize the coming?**

2. Will your neighborhood have conditions or reservations to place on the coming of the Cosmic Christ? What would they be?

3. If your neighborhood welcomed the Cosmic Christ, what would it have to surrender? What would it have to embrace?

4. If your neighborhood welcomed the Cosmic Christ, how will it do so (a ritual, present the key to the city, other ideas)?

Strategy Two
Have the groups present the scenarios that would cause each neighborhood to reconsider its present worldview. Each group will give the background to the scenario and then role-play the responses of different people in the neighborhood.

Other Possibilities

1. After reviewing *The Coming of the Cosmic Christ*, what do you think or feel now about the book compared to your preconceptions about it?
Review people's thoughts and feelings after completing Fox's book.

2. What are your thoughts and feelings on the litany of deliverance on page 244? Would you omit any of the petitions or add other dimensions to it? Why?
Have the participants share their thoughts and feelings on the litany of deliverance. What would they omit or add to it?

3. After reading and studying *The Coming of the Cosmic Christ*, what are your dreams for the future?
Have the participants share their dreams for the future.

Personal Response and Lifestyle Choices
Lead the group to come up with some lifestyle choices as a result of their study of *The Coming of the Cosmic Christ*.

1.   "To what work and what actions does a belief in the Cosmic Christ lead?" (p. 8)

2.   After reviewing *The Coming of the Cosmic Christ*, have each person share what he or she has to surrender or embrace in order to welcome the Cosmic Christ.

3.   What support does each one need from family, friends, church companions, this group and/or others to welcome the Cosmic Christ?

4.   What transformation will each one experience in his or her lifestyle by welcoming the Cosmic Christ?

5.   In response to our deepening knowledge and awareness of the presence of the Cosmic Christ, we will . . .

Closing

Take time to thank the participants for their sharing during the six sessions.

Darken the room, light the candle, and quiet the group. Tell everyone to let the silence surround them.

Begin to pass the globe or galaxy ball. Remind the participants not to hurry.

As participants receive the globe, they can share the hope and vision they have for the world.

Pass the globe a second time; ask each person to commit to making his or her hope and vision a reality: "I commit to making _____ a reality by _____."

After each one has shared, let the silence settle for a minute or two, then turn the lights on.

Alternate Closing: Read the litany of deliverance petitions the group has accepted. If applicable, add the other dimensions the group decided on.

Materials for Group Distribution

Session 1: Our Mother Is Dying

Prologue and part 1 in *The Coming of the Cosmic Christ.*

Opening

Before reading the prologue and part 1, make a list of the expectations and or preconceptions you have regarding Matthew Fox's book *The Coming of the Cosmic Christ.* Include preconceptions you might have about Matthew Fox, as well as expectations you might have for the study of the text itself.

Give your response to Albert Einstein's query, "What is the most important question you can ask in life?"

Getting Into the Text

1. What is your understanding of cosmology, the Enlightenment, and the paradigm shift in Matthew Fox's presentation?

2. In part 1 what evidence does Matthew Fox give to support his vision that Mother Earth is dying? What evidence would you add?

3. With the overemphasis on the analytical and verbal (the left hemisphere of the brain), what does Fox say we have lost?

4. How do you respond to the statement, "The goal of education is not wisdom but getting a job" (p. 22)?

5. Since the word mother is defined in relationship to a child, what ramifications are there for youth if we say, "Your Mother is dying"?

6. What is lost with the passing of native peoples, their religions, and their cultures? Do you agree with Fox's assessment of native peoples?

7. Fox has a severe indictment of Mother Church. Fox uses the term "Mother Church" to refer primarily to the institutionalized Roman Catholic Church, though other institutions might be considered as well. In your own words rephrase this indictment or write your own assessment.

Getting Into the Heart

Reflect on the following quotes. Are there any other quotes that deepened your understanding of the crucifixion of Mother Earth?

Other Titles in Harper's Leader's Guide Series

When the Heart Waits by Sue Monk Kidd

Addiction and Grace by Gerald G. May

Letters to Marc About Jesus by Henri J. M. Nouwen

The Kingdom Within by John A. Sanford

Faith Under Fire by Daniel J. Simundson

Forgive and Forget by Lewis B. Smedes

A Tree Full of Angels by Macrina Wiederkehr

> You can order any of Harper's Leader's Guide Series books through your local bookstore or by writing to Torch Publishing Group, Harper San Francisco, 151 Union Street, Suite 401, San Francisco, CA 94111, or call us toll-free: 800-328-5125.

Healer," "Sexual Mysticism," and others, as well as additional video tapes. For these and *Creation Spirituality Magazine* contact: Friends of Creation Spirituality, PO Box 19216, Oakland, CA 94619.

Hildegarde of Bingen. *Book of Divine Works with Letters and Songs.* Ed. Matthew Fox. Santa Fe: Bear & Company, 1987. This is a presentation of Hildegarde's letters and songs.

Kuhn, Thomas. *The Structure of Scientific Revolutions.* Chicago: University of Chicago Press, 1970. This book gives a more complete explanation of the origins, development, and results of paradigm shifts.

Ruether, Rosemary Radford. *New Woman, New Earth.* San Francisco: Harper & Row, 1984. In this book Ruether critiques patriarchal religion and ideologies, then gives a vision of feminism's transformative response to culture. See also her book *Mary: The Feminine Face of the Church.* Philadelphia: Westminster, 1977.

Schillebeeckx, Edward. *Jesus.* New York: Crossroad, 1979. Schillebeeckx offered an experiment in Christology, using a creation-centered starting point for looking at Jesus' person and message—a move from the traditional fall-redemption presentations. His books *Christ* and *The Church with a Human Face* also use the same starting point.

Additional Resources for Leaders

de Chardin, Teilhard. *Human Energy.* New York: Harcourt Brace Jovanovich, 1969. In this work Teilhard calls for a vision of social transformation according to the spirit of the earth, the one universal spirit of all humankind.

Doyle, Brendan. *Meditations with Julian of Norwich.* Santa Fe: Bear & Company, 1983. This book is a translation of Julian of Norwich's work. Fox recommends this book because of its format for prayer and artistic response to Julian's mystical imagery.

Fox, Matthew. *Original Blessing.* Santa Fe: Bear & Company, 1983. In this book Fox presents the spiritual tradition of Creation Spirituality in its Four Paths and twenty-six themes, a mysticism for the masses, rootedness in original blessing, and the creative response to all life.

_____. *A Spirituality Named Compassion.* San Francisco: Harper & Row, 1990. This book explores compassion, examining its biblical, sexual, psychological, artistic, scientific, political, economic, and symbolic meanings.

_____. *Meditations with Meister Eckhart.* Santa Fe: Bear & Company, 1983. Fox presents Eckhart's spirituality in his own words and arranged for prayer, ritual, artistic, and mystical response.

_____. *Creation Spirituality Magazine.* This bi-monthly magazine, with Matthew Fox as editor-in-chief, examines the Cosmic Christ tradition in today's culture by way of interviews, articles, and stories from around the world. It offers rituals, art as meditation exercises, and "earth notes" to feed the spirit.

_____. *The Cosmic Christ* video presents Matthew Fox in an interview with broadcast journalist Roland Smith discussing themes in *The Coming of the Cosmic Christ* as well as Fox's own personal journey. (It is three parts, 84 minutes total viewing time.) Also available are audio tapes by Fox derived from *The Coming of the Cosmic Christ,* including "The Cosmic Christ as

2. What are your thoughts and feelings on the litany of deliverance on page 244? Would you omit any of the petitions or add another dimension to it? Why?

3. After reading and studying *The Coming of the Cosmic Christ,* what are your dreams for the future?

Personal Response and Lifestyle Choices

1. "To what work and what action does a belief in the Cosmic Christ lead?" (p. 8).

2. After reviewing *The Coming of the Cosmic Christ,* what do you have to surrender or embrace in order to welcome the Cosmic Christ?

3. What support do you need from family, friends, church companions, this group and/or others to welcome the Cosmic Christ?

4. What transformation do you expect to experience in your lifestyle if you welcome the Cosmic Christ?

5. In response to our deepening knowledge and awareness of the presence of the Cosmic Christ, we will . . .

3. Church Decisions (if applicable): Who makes them, how are they made (process, criteria), who is accountable, who affected? Who is welcome or accepted in the church? What is the level of trust? What is it based on?

4. Describe what sexuality, morality, creativity, play, work, and worship look like in the neighborhood. What place does each one have in the life of the people?

5. Describe how the neighborhood feels about the government, the military, social programs.

6. What would cause each neighborhood to reconsider its present worldview.

Strategy One: The Cosmic Christ Is Coming!

If your group has chosen strategy one, you will be asked to discuss these questions. (Use your imagination, creativity, your right brain as well as the content from Fox's presentation to approach these questions.)

1. Will your neighborhood welcome the Cosmic Christ? Why or Why not? What would it take for it to recognize the coming?

2. Will your neighborhood have conditions or reservations to place on the coming of the Cosmic Christ? What would they be?

3. If your neighborhood welcomed the Cosmic Christ, what would it have to surrender? What would they have to embrace?

4. If your neighborhood welcomed the Cosmic Christ, how will it do so (a ritual, present the key to the city, other ideas)?

Strategy Two

If your group has chosen strategy two, you will dramatize scenarios that might cause your neighborhood to reconsider its present worldview. You will need to give background to the scenario and then role-play the responses of different people in the neighborhood.

Other Possibilities

1. Review your "What I Think and Feel" from the five previous sessions. After reviewing *The Coming of the Cosmic Christ,* what do you think or feel now about the book compared to your preconceptions about it.

This discussion guide may be photocopied for local use.

Neighborhood 2: Outer Suburbia

- Mobile neighborhood (3–5 years)
- Moderate income (middle to upper middle)
- Mixed families (single- and two-parent); 1–3 children
- Two incomes usually
- Mixed backgrounds (ethnic, educational, economic, religious, etc.)
- Mixed level of church involvement
- (Add other characteristics to flesh out this neighborhood)

Neighborhood 3: Inner Urban

- Stable neighborhood (feeling of being stuck here by many)
- Lower income level
- Mixed families (leaning toward more single-parent families); 3–8 children
- Usually single income, welfare a reality for many
- Mixed backgrounds—black, Hispanic, and new immigrants with some whites
- For many the church is a respite in a bleak experience, a connection with their mother country; for others it is another oppressor
- (Add other characteristics to flesh out this neighborhood)

Neighborhood 4: Outer Urban

- Mobile neighborhood (many renters)
- Middle to upper middle income, some wealthy
- Mixed lifestyles (single- and two-parent families, homosexual singles and couples)
- Single and double incomes
- Mixed backgrounds (ethnic, educational, economic, religious, etc.)
- Mixed level of church involvement (from alienation to full participation)
- (Add other characteristics to flesh out this neighborhood)

Brainstorm Background Questions (in a real, not ideal, setting)

1. Family Decisions: Who makes them, how are they made (process, criteria), who is accountable, who affected? Who is welcome or acceptable in the family? What is the level of trust? What is it based on?

2. Neighborhood and Civic Decisions: Who makes them, how are they made (process, criteria), who is accountable, who affected? Who is welcome or accepted in the neighborhood or civic community? What is the level of trust? What is it based on?

Session 6: Am I Ready for the Cosmic Christ?

Read the Epilogue and Appendices in *The Coming of the Cosmic Christ*.

Opening
How do you experience the dying of Mother Earth?

Getting Into the Text

1. After your study of Fox's book, write a description of mysticism's place in the coming of the Cosmic Christ.

2. Who is the Cosmic Christ?

3. What paradigm shift do you feel must happen in society and/or the church? Why? Do you think the environment exists for this shift to happen?

4. What is the most important message of the Cosmic Christ for you? Why?

5. What are the ramifications for a person who believes in the Cosmic Christ—lifestyle, education, social and ecumenical responsibilities, and so on. What are the ramifications for a church or society?

Getting Into the Heart
In this section background data is offered for four imaginary but possible neighborhoods. You have been assigned one of these neighborhoods. With it in mind, brainstorm your responses to the background questions.

Neighborhood 1: Inner Suburbia or Rural
- Stable neighborhood (15+ years)
- Moderate income
- Two parents, 3–8+ children
- Husband works outside the home; wife at home; if farm, everyone works
- White
- Churchgoers
- (Add other characteristics to flesh out this neighborhood)

This discussion guide may be photocopied for local use.

"[We] need to 'reinvent the human'" (Thomas Berry in Fox, p. 160).

"We need today a historical Christ—a living Christ who can change history once again and ground that change in a living cosmology" (p. 162).

"How are we treating our young? Are we preparing them to love life? Are we offering them skills and disciplines for adventure, for sacrifice, for great visions to which they can give themselves?" (p. 181).

"Living worship, based on a living cosmology, creates a people and heals a people; it celebrates a people and their amazing place in the universe" (p. 212).

" . . . I'm convinced that the only way to survive nuclear roulette is to stop playing the game, to put down the gun globally, to move beyond war. If we want to avoid the world's imminent suicide, we must shift totally the way we think about war. We no longer can accept it as a means of settling disputes, as an extension of politics or as an innate ingredient in the nature of man" (Martin Heldman in Fox, p. 234).

"Religious traditions hold collective power—especially because they are more in touch with the *anawim* or voiceless ones—to motivate govern- ments to interact on behalf of peace and justice" (p. 235).

"The Cosmic Christ still needs to be born in all of us—no individual, race, religion, culture, or time is excluded. 'Christ' is a generic name. In that sense we are all 'other Christs'" (p. 235).

Personal Response and Lifestyle Choices

1. For me to be another Christ means . . .

2. The deep healing that I believe needs to happen is . . .

3. "To what work and what actions does a belief in the Cosmic Christ lead?" (p. 8).

4. In response to the deepening knowledge and awareness of our being "other Christs," I will . . .

8. Fox states that the Cosmic Christ will awaken "the divine powers of creativity in all persons" (p. 199). Where does he see creativity happening? What part of Fox's presentation on creativity excited you? Why?

9. "What are the personal arts that we all need to start birthing anew?" (p. 200). What value do you put on them?

10. Fox gives six steps to revitalizing worship. Evaluate his list by making "1" least important and "10" very important (vital).

Reset all of worship in a cosmological context.	1.....2.....3.....4.....5.....6.....7.....8.....9.....10
Bring the body back.	1.....2.....3.....4.....5.....6.....7.....8.....9.....10
Bring play back.	1.....2.....3.....4.....5.....6.....7.....8.....9.....10
Make room for Via Negativa, darkness, silence, suffering.	1.....2.....3.....4.....5.....6.....7.....8.....9.....10
Awaken and nurture the prophet.	1.....2.....3.....4.....5.....6.....7.....8.....9.....10
Bring participation back.	1.....2.....3.....4.....5.....6.....7.....8.....9.....10

11. What are the lessons Fox says can be learned from native worship? Would you add these lessons to your steps in revitalizing worship? Why or why not?

12. Fox presents the challenge to bring about deep ecumenism based in mysticism. What do you think are the ramifications of accepting that challenge for world religions, education, and justice?

13. Is the term Cosmic Christ anti-ecumenical?

Getting Into the Heart

Reflect on the meaning of the quotes cited below. Are there any other quotes that deepened your understanding of the healing and renaissance that the Cosmic Christ will bring?

"Both religion and sexuality heal the split between ourselves and the universe. We discover that we are indeed 'part of everything' and one with the mystery of life. To talk about God in relation to our sexuality means to be aware of love moving in us, for 'in God we live and move and have our being'" (Dorothee Soelle in Fox, p. 157).

Session 5: Healing Mother Earth

Read part 5 in *The Coming of the Cosmic Christ.*

Opening

Prepare a creative reflection (dance, body movement, poem, song, etc.) on the healing called for in Walt Whitman's quote, "If life and the soul are sacred the human body is sacred" (in Fox, p. 157).

Getting Into the Text

1. Fox asks, "Is the human race still capable . . . of a new birth from a spiritual initiative?" (p. 160). Mark your response to that question and give your reason.

1..........2..........3..........4..........5..........6..........7..........8..........9..........10

No   Maybe   Yes

2. Fox says that the West's teaching on sexuality has been marked by silence and moralizing, leaving a message of regret. What does he mean by those statements? Do you agree with his assessment?

3. In contrast to the West's teaching on sexuality, Fox presents the sexual mysticism of the Song of Songs. What are the elements of sexual mysticism Fox sees present in the Song of Songs? Do you agree or disagree with the perspective on sexuality in the Song of Songs?

4. Fox states that the female and male actors in the Song of Songs do not play out stereotypical roles. What does he mean by this statement? Do you agree?

5. Fox asserts that the problems with today's youth are caused by adultism (excessive adult self-interest). Rate your agreement with his assertion. Why?

Strongly Disagree   Disagree   Unsure   Agree   Strongly Agree

6. In Section 26 Fox describes modern society as Chronos. What does he mean? What is the role of Christos?

7. In a healthy psyche and culture, *Senex* (the old) and *Puer* (the young) work together. What are the healthy aspects of each? Why are both necessary? Make a two-column chart. Head one column *Senex* and the other *Puer*. Under each, list its healthy aspects.

This discussion guide may be photocopied for local use.

takes place and is passed on; wherever compassion prevails, the Cosmic Christ is healing, redeeming, liberating on a cosmic scale. The Cosmic Christ leads the way to cosmic redemption" (p. 153).

Personal Response and Lifestyle Choices

Use a creative medium to name the Cosmic Christ (poetry, dance, drawing, painting, song, humor, etc.).

1. "To what work and what actions does a belief in the Cosmic Christ lead?" (p. 8).

2. In response to the deepening knowledge and awareness of the "I-am-ness" of the Cosmic Christ, I will . . .

Getting Into the Heart

Reflect on the quotes below. Are there any other quotes that deepened your understanding of the Cosmic Christ?

"Divine am I inside and out, and I make holy whatever I touch or am touched from.

"Why should I wish to see God better than this day?

. . . .

I see something of God each hour of the twenty-four, and each moment then,

In the faces of men and women I see God, and in my own face in the glass;

I find letters from God dropped in the street, and every one is signed by God's name" (Walt Whitman in Fox, p. 130).

"Belief is not belief if it is not launched into *praxis*" (p. 134).

"[. . . because of the incarnation the human is involved] in a new responsibility. He can no longer wriggle out of it on the plea of his littleness and nothingness, for the dark God has slipped the atom bomb and chemical weapons into his hands and given him the power to empty out the apocalyptic vials of wrath on his fellow creatures. Since he has been granted an almost godlike power, he can no longer remain blind and unconscious. He must know something of God's nature and of metaphysical processes if he is to understand himself and thereby achieve gnosis of the Divine" (Carl Jung in Fox, p. 138).

"The earth should not be injured, the earth should not be destroyed. As often as the elements of the world are violated by ill-treatment, so God will cleanse them. God will cleanse them through the sufferings, through the hardships of humankind. All of creation God gives to humankind to use. But if this privilege is misused, God's justice permits creation to punish humanity" (Hildegard of Bingen in Fox, p. 144).

"Salvation is understood as liberation from bondage" (p. 150).

"The Good News we yearn to hear and that Mother Earth herself yearns to feel is that salvation is about solidarity: solidarity with God, neighbor, and all God's creatures. The idea of private salvation is obsolete" (p. 151).

"Our capacity for the universe is both divine and demonic, both positive and negative, both glory and shadow" (p. 152).

"Wherever injustice reigns the Cosmic Christ is crucified again. This also means that wherever justice is fought for and prevails; wherever healing

This discussion guide may be photocopied for local use.

Session 4: The Challenge of the Cosmic Christ

Read part 4 in *The Coming of the Cosmic Christ.*

Opening

Prepare your own list of the titles or names of Jesus Christ. What do you think titles and names do; what are their purposes and power?

Getting Into the Text

1. What are the differences between a mindless (unhealthy) and a mindful (healthy) religion?

2. "How can religion accomplish this task of mindfulness?" (p. 132).

3. Fox names the Cosmic Christ "The Pattern that Connects." What does he mean?

4. Using the new wineskin imagery, Fox says that the new paradigm of the Cosmic Christ ushers in a call for a new lifestyle (a connecting, coherent wineskin). What connections do you see the Cosmic Christ making?

5. Fox says that the Cosmic Christ demands a paradigm shift from one worldview to another. Translate his list into one that relates to your experience. Make a four-column chart. Head the first column *Fox's From . . .*, the second column *Fox's To . . .*, the third column *My From . . .*, and the last, *My To . . . .* Fill in the columns.

Do you understand and accept Fox's list? Do you have any questions or misgivings about it?

6. What do you think Fox means when he says, "The Cosmic Christ is not born yet"?

7. What are the two persons Jesus became for us? What do his followers become?

8. What allusions does Fox use to align Jesus Christ with Mother Earth? What does he hope will ensue from this new symbol?

9. What is the "paschal mystery for the Third Millennium"?

10. Which of the eleven descriptive names Fox gives to the Cosmic Christ resonate in you? Why?

This discussion guide may be photocopied for local use.

"When are we like God? I will tell you.
  In so far as we love compassion and practice it steadfastly,
  to that extent do we resemble the heavenly Creator
  who practices these things ceaselessly in us" (Mechtild in Fox,
    p. 118).

"I saw a great oneing between Christ and us
  because when he was in pain we were in pain.
  All creatures of God's creation that can suffer pain suffered with him.
  The sky and the earth failed at the time of Christ's dying because he
    too was part of nature" (Julian of Norwich in Fox, p. 124).

Personal Response and Lifestyle Choices

Personal Paradigm Shifts
1. Identify a time in your life when you were stopped in your regular routine or relationship patterns. Describe the experience.

2. What new questions arose from the experience? What went amiss?

3. What resulted from the breakdown (failure to fit)?

4. Did you try to hold onto the "old way"? Why or why not?

5. Did you waver between the "old" and "new" ways of responding or relating?

Societal Paradigm Shifts
1. Where in the world or universe are there anomalies (breakdowns) where old answers or practices are not working?

2. What new questions do these anomalies raise for you?

3. How do you think a belief in the Cosmic Christ might address these experiences?

4. What does the Cosmic Christ call for in these experiences?

Lifestyle Choices
1. "To what work and what actions does a belief in the Cosmic Christ lead?" (p. 8).

2. In response to the deepening knowledge and awareness I have gained from the study of *The Coming of the Cosmic Christ,* I will . . .

7. Drawing from the biblical, patristic, and medieval sources, come up with your own description of the Cosmic Christ.

8. Make a two -column chart. Label one column *Historical Jesus* and the other *Cosmic Christ.* Write their particular characteristics in the appropriate column.

Getting Into the Heart

Some selections from Scripture and mystic literature that touch on the Cosmic Christ are listed below. Reflect on them and the others that Fox presents. Which ones deepened your understanding of the Cosmic Christ? Were there any that you had questions about?

"'Am I a God close at hand, and not a God far off?' says the Lord. 'Can anyone hide oneself in secret places where I shall not see them? Do I not fill heaven and earth?' says the Lord" (Jer. 23:23–24).

"The word of Yahweh was addressed to me, saying, 'Before I formed you in the womb I knew you, before you came to birth I consecrated you; I have appointed you a prophet to the nations'" (Jer. 1:4–5).

"He is the image of the invisible God, the first-born of all creation; for in him all things were created, in heaven and on earth, visible and invisible, whether thrones or dominions or principalities or authorities—all things were created through him and for him. He is before all things, and in him all things hold together. He is the first-born from the dead, that in everything he might be preeminent. For in him all the fullness of God was pleased to dwell, and through him to reconcile to himself all things, whether on earth or in heaven, making peace by his death on the cross" (Col. 1:15–20).

"In the beginning was the Word:the Word was with God and the Word was God. This Word was with God in the beginning. Through it all things came to be, not one thing had its being but through it. All that came to be had life in it . . . ." (John 1:1–4).

"God became a human being in order that human beings might become God" (Iranaeus in Fox, p. 109).

"The Logos of God has become human so that you might learn from a human being how a human being may become divine" (Clement of Alexandria in Fox, p. 109).

"Every creature participates in some way in the likeness of the Divine Essence" (Thomas Aquinas in Fox, p. 115).

This discussion guide may be photocopied for local use.

Session 3: Questing for the Cosmic Christ

Read part 3 in *The Coming of the Cosmic Christ.*

Opening

What comes to mind when you hear "new wine in old skins," or "new wine in fresh skins"?

Getting Into the Text

1. Describe what Fox feels the Enlightenment and Augustine have bequeathed to the people of the West.

2. In the quest for the Cosmic Christ what paradigms or worldviews does Fox say we have to get rid of? What does this mean to you, and how do you feel about it?

3. Weight Kuhn's descriptions of the new paradigm ("10" being the one that best expresses your experience of vision or life shifts in your own life and "1" being the one that least expresses it). Give your reasons for your choices.

See nature in a new way	1...2...3...4...5...6...7...8...9...10
A shift of vision	1...2...3...4...5...6...7...8...9...10
A transformation of vision	1...2...3...4...5...6...7...8...9...10
A conversion	1...2...3...4...5...6...7...8...9...10
A map or director for making a map	1...2...3...4...5...6...7...8...9...10
A switch in a visual gestalt	1...2...3...4...5...6...7...8...9...10

4. According to Kuhn what is the process of shifting from one worldview to another? What is required for people involved in a paradigm shift?

5. What are the six categories that alert you to the presence of the Cosmic Christ? Choose one of the texts that Fox suggests (infancy narratives, transfiguration, resurrection, etc.—see pp. 99–107) and reread this Scripture in light of these six categories. What has happened to your understanding and awareness of the events in Jesus' life?

6. After reading sections 16–19, what was your familiarity with the literature from the Wisdom or Cosmic Christ Tradition: very familiar, somewhat familiar, or unfamiliar.

This discussion guide may be photocopied for local use.

Personal Response and Lifestyle Choices

Take time this week to tap the mystic in you by exploring one or more of the following everyday and extraordinary experiences. Write your musings about your mystical being-ness in a journal or notebook.

Everyday Experiences Seen Differently

1. Eating and drinking: Go without water for twenty-four hours. Then experience the awe on drinking your first sip of water.

2. Driving to work or carpooling: Pause before you start, to put your commute in another perspective (moving forward, being on a journey, connecting with others on the road, etc.).

3. Routine experiences: Pause before you begin to work or to do something you always do but which has ceased to energize you, focus your senses and your heart on seeing something new—prepare yourself to be surprised.

Extraordinary Experiences

1. Go to a park and swing.

2. Pause to wonder at creation—a leaf, a tree, a sunset, your hand, and so on. Draw it, paint it, put it in clay, or write a poem about it.

3. Come up with your own creative or mystic response to your week.

Deepening Lifestyle Choices

1. "To what work and what actions does a belief in the Cosmic Christ lead?" (p. 8).

2. In response to the deepening knowledge and awareness I have gained from the study of *The Coming of the Cosmic Christ,* I will . . .

This discussion guide may be photocopied for local use.

Feminist	1...2...3...4...5...6...7...8...9...10
Panentheistic	1...2...3...4...5...6...7...8...9...10
Birthing Images	1...2...3...4...5...6...7...8...9...10
Silence	1...2...3...4...5...6...7...8...9...10
Nothingness and Darkness	1...2...3...4...5...6...7...8...9...10
Childlike Playfulness	1...2...3...4...5...6...7...8...9...10
Psychic Justice	1...2...3...4...5...6...7...8...9...10
Prophetic	1...2...3...4...5...6...7...8...9...10
Being-With-Being	1...2...3...4...5...6...7...8...9...10
True Self	1...2...3...4...5...6...7...8...9...10
Globally Ecumenical	1...2...3...4...5...6...7...8...9...10

7. How can we test mystical claims to discern whether they are authentic or bogus? How would you apply Fox's list of tests?

8. How is the historical Jesus both Mystic and Teacher of Mysticism?

Getting Into the Heart

Reflect on the quotes below. Are there any other quotes from part 2 that deepened your understanding of mysticism?

"The mystic lies deep in every person" (p. 44).

"Never devoid of mystical energy and yearnings, a society that denies the mystic and lacks a prophetic religion to insist on the primary role of the mystic within every psyche and every community, will fall into various forms of pathological pseudo-mysticisms" (p. 46).

"It remains for those who have been touched by the power of religious faith to love religion enough to criticize it" (p. 53).

"Healthy mysticism is panentheistic (all things in God and God in all things)" (p. 57).

"A prophet is a mystic in action" (p. 63).

"Without mysticism there will be no 'deep ecumenism,' no unleashing of the power of wisdom from *all* the world's religious traditions" (p. 65).

This discussion guide may be photocopied for local use.

Session 2: Resurrection Through Mysticism

Read part 2 in *The Coming of the Cosmic Christ.*

Getting Into the Text

1. When you hear the word mystic, what images come to mind?

2. On a sheet of paper make a two-column chart. Head one column *Fall-Redemption* and another one *Creation-Centered Original Blessing.* Under each column head list the characteristics of each according to Fox. Then add your own comments, interpretations, and questions under each column.

3. What are the effects of denying the mystic?

4. Fox describes mysticism as "the shadow side of the Western person." What do you think he means by this?

5. On another sheet list the heads *Pseudo-Mysticism, Today's Examples,* and *Healthy Mysticism.* Give examples of each.

6. Fox offers twenty-one running definitions, working definitions, of mysticism. Beside each one mark your level of experience (1=never experienced, 5=faintly experienced, 10=strongly experienced). Write your own understanding of each one.

Experience	1...2...3...4...5...6...7...8...9...10
Nondualism	1...2...3...4...5...6...7...8...9...10
Compassion	1...2...3...4...5...6...7...8...9...10
Connection-Making	1...2...3...4...5...6...7...8...9...10
Radical Amazement	1...2...3...4...5...6...7...8...9...10
Affirmation of the World as a Whole	1...2...3...4...5...6...7...8...9...10
Right Brain	1...2...3...4...5...6...7...8...9...10
Self-Critical	1...2...3...4...5...6...7...8...9...10
Heart Knowledge	1...2...3...4...5...6...7...8...9...10
A Return to the Source	1...2...3...4...5...6...7...8...9...10

Let your hearts be broken, not your garments torn.'
Turn to Yahweh your God again,
for Yahweh is all tenderness and compassion" (Joel 2:12–13).

Second Voice (hopeful):
"There is still hope, there is still something we can do to turn things
around, to convert and change our ways" (Fox, p. 34).

First Voice (full of promise):
"'After this
I will pour out my spirit on all humankind.
Your sons and daughters shall prophesy,
your old folks shall dream dreams
and your young ones see visions.
Even on the slaves, men and women,
will I pour out my spirit in those days.
I will display portents in heaven and on earth
blood and fire and columns of smoke.' The sun will be turned into
darkness,
and the moon into blood,
before the day of Yahweh dawns,
that great and terrible day" (Joel 2:28–31).

Second Voice:
"In this book I call for a new Pentecost, a coming of the messianic
spirit to the entire human race and all its religions and cultures. But
I also call for penance, a deep and radical self-criticism and letting
go especially among my own people" (Fox, pp. 5–6).

Guided Reflection

To be read aloud by two group members.

First Voice (with awe and power):
"In the beginning God created the heavens and the earth. Now the earth was a formless void, there was darkness over the deep, and God's spirit hovered over the waters.
God said, "Let there be..." and God saw that it was good.
God created humans in the image of God,
male and female God created them.
God saw all that was made, and indeed it was very good" (Gen. 1; a paraphrase).

Second Voice:
"We belong to the ground
It is our power
And we must stay close to it
Or maybe we will get lost" (Narritjin Maymuru Yirrkala in Fox, p. 11).

First Voice (tone of lamentation):
"Stand dismayed, you farmers, wail, you vinedressers, for the wheat, for the barley; the harvest of the field has been ruined. The vine has withered, the fig tree wilts away; pomegranate, and palm, and apple, every tree in the field is drooping. Yes, gladness has faded among the sons and daughters of the human race" (Joel 1:11–12).

Second Voice (tone of lamentation):
Mother Earth is dying.
The mystical brain is dying.
Creativity is dying. Wisdom is dying.
The youth are dying.
Native peoples, their religions, and cultures are dying.
Mother Church is dying. Mother love is dying.
We are dying.

First Voice (tone of hope):
"'But now, now'—it is Yahweh who speaks—
'come back to me with all your heart,
fasting, weeping, mourning.

This exercise may be photocopied for local use.

"How full of vitality are we these days? And how full of vitality are our institutions of worship, education, politics, economics?" (p. 2).

"What is needed if there is to be a twenty-first century for Mother Earth and her children is a spiritual vision that prays, celebrates, and lives out the reality of the Cosmic Christ who lives and breathes in Jesus and in *all* God's children, in all the prophets of religions everywhere, in all creatures of the universe" (p. 7).

"God is both mother and father, but God is more mother than father" (p. 34).

"What does it take to bring the healthy mother back to balance with the healthy father in us all?" (p. 34).

"Am I my mother's keeper?" (p. 33).

Personal Response and Lifestyle Choices

1. "To what work and what actions does a belief in the Cosmic Christ lead?" (p. 8).

2. In response to the new knowledge and awareness I have gained from the study of part 1, I will . . .